INSPIRATIONAL HUGS FOR LIVING

Volume II of Live to Learn

and Learn to Live

MIRRON NOBLE

3G Publishing, Inc.

Loganville, Ga 30052

www.3gpublishinginc.com

Phone: 1-888-442-9637

First published by 3G Publishing, Inc. June, 2023.

ISBN: 9781941247037

Contents

Introduction

You are about to receive a hug for every venture of your life. Also, sprinkled throughout this Volume II of "Live to Learn and Learn to Live" are more "Tried and True Nuggets of Wisdom." Together the hugs and the nuggets will cause you to smile, laugh, have wonderful thoughts and memories, and warm and fuzzy feelings inside!

So sit back and get ready to be pampered inspirationally for the rest of your life's journey.

Foreword

In Volume I of Inspirational Hugs For Living, we learned how to "Live to Learn and Learn to Live." In this second volume, you will experience a virtue that makes all that you have learned about life and living worth all that it was meant to be!

So my question to you is, "Have you ever just wanted or needed a hug?" Of course you have we all have!

As you cuddle up and stroll through Inspirational Hugs For Living, that is exactly what you will receive. Hugs whether physical or inspirational meet a need that no other resource can supply or fulfill. They speak a universal language that is not taught from a textbook.

It is a natural virtue created inside of each of us that is activated from birth. When a mother is introduced to her newborn, she without a moment's thought reaches out her two arms to embrace and hug her brand new human being. From that moment on we desire and welcome hugs and the comfort, joy, love, and peace that they bring!

So Hug More...

Dedication

This book is dedicated to YOU...The Reader. Every word is signed, sealed, delivered, and inspired by God, from me to you. It is just another way that God pours His love into each of us!

Happy Hugs and Much Love from God, to me, to you!

TO GOD BE THE GLORY

~Hugs~

You ever wonder why God gave us two arms

He could have just as easily created us with one

But I truly believe one of the reasons that He gave us two

Is so that I could use them when you need a hug

To wrap them around you

#Give a hug
#Ecclesiastes 3:5

~All about God and Evie~

I have a little granddaughter whose name is Evelyn Elaine

Those of us in the family call her Evie

She is the only child of my son, Stephen

One day the enemy tried to take her out

But God worked a miracle and that is without a doubt

Even though we didn't understand

Why that tumor was in her brain

One thing I do know is that nothing for Him is too large or small

What seems impossible to man

Is Just Right for God!!!

#09-09-19
#God did it for Evie
#He can do it for you
#Thank you God for hugging us with a miracle!!!

~Babies in Heaven~

I have a baby girl who is now in Heaven with the Lord

He took her with Him while she was yet in my womb, so she was still-born

I had a chance to cradle her in my arms and for a short time look upon her angelic face

So now I will be able to recognize her when I too get to Heaven some day!

#Dedicated to all mothers who have Babies in Heaven
#My Baby Girl was born August 14, 1975
#So glad I was able to hug her!!!

~The Doctor~

I often wonder where that Doctor could be today

Who promised me by my bedside he would stay

He even offered and said that I could squeeze his hand

Every time that I had one of those very hard labor pains

I was only in my early 20s when this took place

Oh but now I realize that this Doctor was God's Amazing Grace

I'm in my late 60s now but I shall never forget

The Doctor who at my bedside I met!

#Happened August 14, 1975
#Giving birth to my second child
#Met the Doctor
#That child was stillborn
#God was hugging me even then
#Written August 5, 2022

~The Children~

The Bible tells us that children are a blessing from the Lord

That is why Jesus said, "Suffer them to come unto me and forbid them not,"

For truly He loves them all

I am so thankful for the children that He entrusted to me

I've tried to be a good steward over them both naturally and spiritually

Make sure that you as parents give them both quality and quantity of your time

Trust me, whatever you sow into them will come back up the same kind

So train the children up in the way that they should go

Because Jesus cares for and loves the children for the Bible tells us so!

#Give your children lots of Hugs!
#They will hug you back some day!

~Thankfulness vs. Gratefulness~

You can't tell someone "thank you" too many times

For no one has to be, plus you can't repay them for being kind

So if you are really thankful you should put it into words

Because it makes the person feel appreciated when these words are heard

But on the other hand gratefulness is best when it is put into action

Otherwise you will be the only one who receives feelings of satisfaction

So the only way that the other person will truly know that you are grateful

You must show it in deeds and not words only!

#Tell someone thank you
#Show them you're GRATEFUL
#Give them a hug!

~Love and Kindness~

When you visit the home of Love and Kindness

You will never want to leave

What your eyes behold

You can hardly believe

Love treats Kindness like a queen

And Kindness treats Love like a king

It is the most romantic relationship that you have ever seen

I simply cannot imagine one without the other

My prayer for them is that they will be together eternally!!

~Less Is More~

Less becomes more when you're trying to enter Heaven's door

Your decrease will turn into increase when you learn that more of yourself you must release

When you leave this earth, you will take nothing with you

So learn to give yourself away

And live with less and less each and every day!

#Give more hugs!
#And they will come back to you!

~ What Are You Wearing ~

The fragrance of a smile

That will linger for miles

Will make a lasting statement

A genuine show of love

Designed especially by the Creator above

Will leave an impression on many for days to come

Choose what you wear carefully

Remember people are watching you daily

Most importantly dress from the inside out

That's how the world will know what you're truly all about!

#Look at you!

~Happy Birthday~

Birthdays are very special

A celebration second to none

As we reflect back over our lives

From the day that we were born

I truly thank God for each and every one

For all that He has brought me through

I look forward to friends and family saying

"Happy Birthday To You!"

It seems as though I've become happier with each passing year

I believe it's because I've come to appreciate life more as

I Live to Learn and Learn to Live!

#Written on my birthday, July 7, 2018
#Happy Birthday To Me!
#64

~*Good Morning!*~

Something about the morning is so intriguing

It's like receiving a special invitation with an RSVP that causes you to be filled with excitement

Wait a minute, are those birds that I hear singing

They're up awfully early this morning with a Good Morning Greeting

The morning will be Good no matter what happened the night before

Because God promised that it would bring Joy

Oh my goodness, is that a present with a note,

Signed: From God to Me

And it's full of Brand New Mercies

I can hardly wait to open it up and see!

#Good Morning!

~Oh Happy Day~

Another day has come and gone, twenty-four hours have passed our way

If that day could speak, I wonder what it would say

Would it say that you greeted him with a word repeated from what the Lord said

Or did he hear you grumbling and complaining about getting up on the wrong side of the bed

A day is a gift to us, directly from the Lord

We should be very Happy and begin each one gladly and Rejoice!!!

#Each new day is a hug from the Lord!

~Dancing~

Dancing is a language spoken by the feet!

It really starts in the heart with each and every beat!

#A good hug will cause you to want to dance!

~Real Love~

Some imitations are so close to the real

That you can hardly tell the difference

Put the two side by side

And you won't know the fake from the genuine

But its totally not that way with Real Love

You can feel it miles away when you can't see it with your eyes

Because it is made in the factory of your heart!

#A hug with love…nothing like it!

~Quiet Strength~

Strength doesn't always have to make a lot of noise

I've learned that it's at its best when it remains reserved and poised!

#Strength is as strength does
#It takes more strength to maintain your poise than to make a lot of noise
#A hug can impart quiet strength!

~Wounded Beauty~

What, you may ask, is the secret to maintaining your beauty after going through life's traumas

A makeup artist is not the answer because no amount of makeup can cover life's disasters

You see the secret dwells on the inside where true beauty resides

So the more you're wounded, the more your beauty will shine!

~Call It A Day~

Some people call it twenty-four hours of work and play,

Taking no time to stop and smell the flowers

Some call it from sun up to sun down

No rest for the weary to be found

But I think I will call it what the Creator said

I call it, "The Day that the Lord has made!"

~I Felt That~

I felt that something was wrong

I had been in this storm seem like much too long

The abundance of tears I shed had washed out my tracks

Even though I thought about it, there was no turning back

Then I heard the words of Jesus say, "I Am The Way"

"I need you my child on this path to stay"

"There is someone on this journey that I need you to meet"

"After you've gone through, they will need your strength!"

#You will meet someone who really needs a hug…!

~Blessed With A Tickle~

My mother possessed a "dry sense of humor."
That is probably where I inherited mine.

Often times when she was telling a story or recalling a memory, she would burst out in laughter!
As is oftentimes with listeners of one with a dry sense of humor, we would look at her in amazement, wondering what was so funny. I often get that as well!

But when my mother would get this look, her response would be, "I tickle myself!" And guess what, I have found myself saying the same thing!

But here recently, after God reveals something to me that inspires me or downloads words of wisdom to me, I find myself smiling and laughing telling God, "God you tickle me!"

So after some thought I asked God, "What is a tickle?" He explained it to me this way. A tickle is like an appetizer before a meal. It satisfies you until the meal comes. So when God tickles us, it is a blessing before the blessing because if the tickle satisfies me, I can't imagine what the meal God has prepared will be like!

#I Corinthians 2:9

~The Lion And The Lamb~

#Based on a true story and inspired by real characters!

One day the lion and the lamb were taking a walk

Said the lamb to the lion, "Let's have a nice talk"

The lion replied, "I don't see any need or have time for all of that

I find I get more results and faster when I roar loudly and attack back!"

The lamb replied, "I don't really see how that can be

I'd rather handle things quietly and peaceably!"

"Well," said the lion, "if you ever need things done in a hurry

Just let me know, I'll relieve you of your worry"

"Alright," replied the lamb, "and if you ever need someone to talk to

Just give me a roar, and I'll be there for you!"

~Moral of the Story~

Just because we are all different does not mean that we can't get along and help each other out!

#I need you and you need me!
#Can we all just get along
#Sometimes hugs come from those who are completely different from us!

~Happiness and Loneliness~

One day Happiness and Loneliness were having a serious conversation.

So Happiness asked Loneliness a question. "Which one of us do you think people would choose if they could only pick one of us?" Mind you, Happiness had already pretty much assumed that even Loneliness' answer would be him, Happiness, because he is always running into people who are crying and complaining about how unhappy they are and how they just wished they could be happy!

So surely Happiness thought that Loneliness' answer would be Happiness. Loneliness pondered over the question for quite a while and took his time before he answered Happiness. For you see that is what lonely people do. They take a long time to think about things before they respond.

"Well," said Loneliness, finally. "I too come across a lot of people who would pick you, Happiness, because they always find themselves for some reason or another being unhappy. But it seems to me that their happiness never lasts very long because as soon as their circumstances change, they are right back where they started!"

"So for that reason," said Loneliness, "I would say more people would pick me because lonely people always take their time before they jump at a chance for happiness!"

#What're your thoughts
#A story with an unexpected ending!

~What's On The Back Burner?~

What is that on the back burner

It's something good that God is preparing for me, but I think it needs turning

God made it with His own secret recipe

Because He knows what it takes to make the best out of me

I've been simmering on the back burner for quite some time

When I asked Him about it, He said, "Don't worry, you will be just fine"

Right when I thought I was about to burn

He said, "Hold on, you're almost done"

So he allowed the devil to stick a fork in me

Only to discover that I was just how God wanted me to be

"Well done," said the Lord, "my good and faithful servant"

"I can now turn off the heat and take you off the back burner!

~Distorted In The Translation~

Throughout the years of your life, God will move you from place to place

Some places that you find yourself in, you were never meant to stay

41

For in some places if you remain there too long

You will grow roots and too comfortable you will become

Then when your time is up and God tries to take you out

You will kick and scream without a doubt

The more you do that, the harder for you it will be

You will cause yourself to be distorted in the translation and miss a God appointed opportunity!

~Holding On Vs. Hanging In There~

When you're going through life's situations,

Some people will tell you to hold on while others will say hang on in there

Well my question is which one do I do, which one do I dare

Is there really a difference or are they one in the same

Let me ponder a moment over this thing

After giving it some thought, I decided to choose holding on instead of just hanging in there

You see if I'm just hanging there, that will get me nowhere

But if I'm holding on, there's a lot that I can hold on to

While at the same time, I'm moving along

I can hold on to faith and trust that I'm going to come out and make it through

But if I'm just hanging in there, I'm motionless in the problem

And will probably end up remaining in it too!

#Hold on and keep on moving on

~But God~

Dialogue based on actual happenings

God: I am about to allow you to go through something that you won't fully understand

Us: But God???

God: Don't worry, I will never leave you or forsake you

Us: But God???

God: Trust ME, all of it will work together for your good…you trust me, don't you

Us: Well yes, but God??

– Long Pause –

After some time of struggle, we finally surrender to God's will and way for us!

Us: God! Thank You for taking me through and bringing me out. You are true to your WORD! I had thought that I would have fainted at one point…..BUT GOD!!!.....

~Creatures of Habit~

Creatures of habit like to play strictly by the rules

They'd rather not change, touch it, or from their old ways move

They live by the motto, "If it's not broke don't fix it"

They believe that sooner or later it will work out eventually

Poor creatures of habit are only stuck in a rut

They miss out on so much more in life that is outside of their little box

If they were ever to take a chance and try something different and new

They will find out there are so much more exciting things in this world to do!

#A reforming creature of habit
#need more work

~It's All Good!~

Maybe right now, things are not going as they should.

But, It's All Good!

You would if you could, change your present situation…

But, It's All Good!

Every time you turn around, something else has turned upside down…

But, It's All Good!

What makes it all good, is God!

He takes everything that you have gone through from the very start

And mixes it all together because He knows you love Him with all of your heart

And what you end up with is something so, sooo good that you can hardly believe

It's the very desire of your heart plus something that you really, really need!

#mmm, mmm Good
#God is Good all the time
#All the time God is Good

~Do Not Disturb~

Please do not disturb, can't you see

I'm relaxing and enjoying the blessings that God has given to me

I'm just resting in the care and love of my Lord

After going through things in life that were very hard

So now He has sent me on this Heavenly Vacation

Ooo chile, do not disturb me

I'll get back with you later!

~Gracefully Broken~

Anything that is broken in our lives

God is able to fix

Even though it doesn't happen when we want it

Because there are some things that He chooses not to completely take away

But His Grace is sufficient to sustain us day by day!

~Location, Location, Location~

It's so important that we're at the right place at the right time

So that when God opens a door for us, we won't be hard to find

I'm not just talking about geographically

But most importantly is mentally

You could very well miss out if you're not thinking like you should

So make very sure your mind has not taken a vacation

Because with God it's all about location, location, location

~Share The Road~

You will share the road with many as you travel along life's way

So be prepared to meet and assist them as you go from day to day

Some you will run into at an intersection

Please don't run on by but yield the right of way and see if they need directions

There will be many that you'll find stranded along the side of the road

Slow down and be prepared to stop and help them with their heavy load

You will run into some that life has burnt out and they arc low on gas

Take the time to let them know that this too shall pass

So don't be selfish in this life's race

But look out for your sister and brother and we will all arrive by God's grace!

~Good Entertainment~

Hey! Don't entertain that negative thought

Grab the remote, change the channel and bring it to a halt

Don't let gossip pull up a chair in your mind

While what "he said and she said" is dancing around in your head having a good time

Instead entertain yourself by thinking on things that are honest, loving, and pure

Now that's some Good Entertainment

I can hardly wait for Part Two!

#Philippians 4:8

~Quick And In A Hurry~

Quick and In A Hurry are always bumping heads

Both want to be first at everything, never considering the other one instead

They're always trying to outrun and outdo each other

They continue to fail to realize that they are both brothers with the same birth mother

If they would only learn to pay more attention and stop wasting time

There would be no need for either of them to always be trying to catch up and not get left behind!

#slow down
#haste makes waste
#do things on time

~Wait~

Hello, my friend, Wait is waiting on you

He's at the very same place he was the last time
that you rushed by him and passed through

He noticed that you were very frantic and disturbed

But he couldn't understand why if you were waiting on the Lord

You see the Lord is never late and He is always on
time

Plus Wait has the patience of Job and worrying is
the farthest thing from his mind

So be encouraged, my friend, and give Wait a
chance

If you do, what you don't see now, you will later
understand!

#Wait on the Lord
#Be of good courage
#Wait, I say on the Lord

~A Wounded Friend~

An offended and wounded friend

Does not always bring the relationship to an end

But when that friend begins to emotionally bleed

That's showing you what they really need!

#A friend in need is truly a friend indeed
#Give and receive more hugs!

~I've Got A Reason To Praise God~

I've got a reason to praise God

When I think of all He's done for me, it's not hard at all

Just remembering makes me clap my hands and break out in a dance

The devil can't stop me, he doesn't even stand a chance

And even if he tries, I'll just lift up my voice

I will sing, rejoice, and make a joyful noise!

~A Picture No Artist Can Draw~

A picture that no artist can draw

Must be the most beautiful thing that you ever saw

I guess that we can only imagine

Until we get to that place called HEAVEN!

~Keep Moving~

Sickness and pain

      Keep Moving!

Sunshine or rain

      Keep Moving!

Death and disaster

      Keep Moving!

And no matter what comes after

      JUST KEEP MOVING!

~I Don't Care~

"I don't care" is a phrase used loosely

Sad and lonely must have been the one who produced it

Because struggles in life make you more caring

Not just about yourself but for everyone else!

#A hug is a good way to show that you really care!

~Swept OFF My Feet~

God has a place to take each of us

A secret place, where trust and obedience are a must

After these requirements we finally meet

With His Love and Grace, He will sweep us off our feet!

~I Have Not~

I have not gone through anything that God didn't bring me out

I have never been left wondering, what was that
all about

I have never been disappointed when I put all my
trust in Him

I have not and will not doubt my God ever again!

~True Colors~

True colors can sometimes be difficult to see

Everything and everybody is not always what they
appear to be

But there is one color that I am sure will never
change

It's the color red, the same color of the blood that
runs from my Savior's veins!

~Be Proactive~

What does being proactive really mean

Simply putting into action those things about
which you have already dreamed!

~In The Middle~

In the middle of trouble

Expect and see yourself coming out with double

When you're in the middle of the pain

Start thanking God for strength and break out in a dance!

Are you in the middle of something and you don't know what it's all about?

Right there is where you should lift your voice and give a VICTORY SHOUT!

When you're in the middle of heartaches and sorrows

That's a good place to believe that things will be much better tomorrow

The beginning can be good and the ending is unseen

But it's in the middle that you become determined that you are coming out

And that you will surely win!

#Don't wait til the battle is over
#Shout in the MIDDLE!

~You Can't Fight Kindness~

You ever wonder why people who are kind wear a smile

They leave behind the memory of it as long as a mile

Kindness has a way of turning bitter into sweet

It will conquer any conflict

It just can't be beat!

#Ephesians 4:32

~The Pain Of The Past~

The pain of the past is never meant to last

It's entirely up to you and how you learn from what you've gone through

Every pain has a purpose,

But it's not for you to forever suffer

Moving on and learning from it is the remedy

Or the pain of the past will forever be your enemy!

~Seize The Moment~

Seize the moment and hold on to it tight

Don't let it go, oh no, not without a fight

When you grab hold of that moment of peace

Seize it with all of your might and don't you dare release

Whatever moment of blessing God sees fit to send your way

Seize that moment before it slips away!

#Seize the moment and hug it tightly!

~Make God Laugh!~

You want to know how to make God laugh

Just let the devil come after you

Thinking he can block you from going through

This always makes God laugh so very hard

That it shakes up the devil's plans until they all fall apart

So just trust and obey God in all that you go through

And make Him laugh at the devil and all that he's trying to do!!!

#HaHa devil
#God gets the last laugh
#Psalms 2:4
#Psalms 59:8

~Save the Date~

Save the date and patiently wait

Your time and season won't be late

God has it circled in RED on His calendar

His plans for you are soooo spectacular

That is why it seems as if it's taking so long

It will absolutely blow your mind when it finally comes!

~There's Always More~

There's always more to what you see

A blessing in disguise it could possibly be!

#you just never know

~Don't Wait~

Don't wait until your grave is green

I know you're wondering, what in the world does that mean

Don't put off til tomorrow what you can do today

For sooner or later in a grave you will lay

After a while green grass will grow over it, and it will be too late

So get busy doing what you should, please don't hesitate!

~Making Sense~

Having a sense of accomplishment simply means
having sense enough to accomplish something
that makes sense!

#Does that make sense???
#Lol!!

~I'm Just Saying~

You never know what God has in store for you…

    I'm Just Saying

Could be something that's really going to bless
you after you've gone through…

    I'm Just Saying

You could have a great testimony after the test…

    I'm Just Saying

You could come out and end up with some of
God's very BEST!

    I'm Just Saying

#IJS

~Enjoy Every Moment~

Please don't allow life to pass you by

In case you didn't know I'm here to tell you why

Because we only have one life to live and no matter what it brings

Whether challenging or easy, always find a reason to sing

So enjoy every moment because you never know from moment to moment what life will bring!

~Keep The Fire Burning~

Let love be your matches

And burn up hate until it becomes ashes

Keep the fire of love forever burning

Until it's no chance of hate ever returning!

#Romans 12:9-10
#Romans 13:10

~Celebrate~

Celebrate the things that made you cry

Don't stop dancing because you don't understand why

Throw a party and celebrate life

Just in case some things might last for a while!

#Make the best of Every Season of Your Life
#Ecclesiastes 3:1-4

~Made in Heaven~

We often talk about things being made in Heaven

But do we really think about where the materials come from

Could it be that they come from prayers sent up to Heaven from a father or mother

Who prayed countless prayers, shipped off with tears

And kept them going up over many many years

Or perhaps a friend stood in the gap for another friend

By supplying intercessions and supplications to the throne room over and over again

So whatever you do, don't stop sending up the prayer timber

Because it's being used to make something in Heaven!

#Matthew 6:10
#Matthew 16:19

~I Made Myself~

I made myself smile

Even when I was messed up inside

I made myself keep trying

Even though I really felt like I was dying

I made myself appear to be glad

When deep down inside I felt extremely sad

Then one day I decided to make myself

Pray Until Something Happened

After a while I realized that I didn't have to make myself pray anymore,

It just happened naturally!

#Prayer changes things and you too
#James 5:16-18
#Make yourself PUSH
#Pray Until Something Happens

~It Is What It Is!~

Some things and people will never change

Before they do, you will be the one they blame

So if you happen to run across someone like this

And this is the way it appears

Just remember that it is what it is!

#Shaking My Head
#SMH

~Cure For Depression~

Depression, my friend, is a very terrible thing

Its goal is to press the very life out of you and rob you of your joy and desire to merrily sing

But I'm not here to diagnose the problem but to give you the cure

There is a remedy for it, of that I am very sure

You must first apply and plead The Blood of Jesus over it

And the same way it came, send it back to Satan and his pit

And just in case it tries to come back

Resist that enemy and it will flee

And that will stop it in its tracks!

~Speak God's Word~

Many things in life will push you to the edge

But there is something in God's word to talk you off that ledge

When life says you can't

God's word says you can

God has thoughts of you and an expected plan

So don't you dare think about jumping off that ledge

Just acknowledge Him in all your ways

And He will direct your path!

#Don't leap, speak God's word
#Say what Jesus said
#Speak before you leap

~Praise the Lord~

You ever wonder why God gave us two hands

Maybe so we could have instruments for our own Praise The Lord Band

Then He turned around and gave us two feet

So come on now, let's Praise The Lord and get on beat!

And a one…and a two…PRAISE THE LORD!!!

#Let everything that has breath, Praise The Lord!

~EASE US JESUS~

We Need Your Help Oh God

      EASE US JESUS!

Oh God Help Us

      Ease Us JESUS!

Help Lord

      ease us JESUS!

Thank You

      JESUS!!!

#Thank God for Jesus
#It Gets Easier with Jesus
#Wisdom Word Trivia

~Free~

There once was a sign that hung out on a tree

The sign read, "A Brand New Life, FREE, if you only believe"

Many eyes gazed upon that sign

And they began to wonder and ponder in their minds

For you see the tree was rugged and the sign was beaten and dirty

Surely they thought, the offer wasn't worth it

After a few hours had passed, still hung that sign, written on it FREE

And it hung there until all of a sudden the whole world changed drastically….

F – Forgiveness

R – Redemption

E – Everyone

E – Everlasting

#*The Rest Is HISTORY*

~Jesus Knows~

Jesus, our Savior, knows how it is to

Stay awake all night

To be on your knees, crying out to the Father

To make everything alright

He, Himself, did it oftentimes, even on His way to the cross

Pleading, Father "please remove this cup"

But later understood it was not the Father's will that the world be lost

Jesus knows how it is and He truly understands

Because not only is He Divine but He lived on this earth as a real man!

#John 3:16

~*Let Me See*~

Let me see if there's still some pain from the past

Nope, it's all gone

God had told me that it wouldn't last

Let me see if I still remember what made me cry

No, it's gone too

Oh well bye-bye

Let me see if my future looks much better than my past

Oh yes! God just gave me a glimpse

And it's much better and it's coming fast!

~I Would Rather Be Me~

I would rather be me than anyone else

Because I have actually become pretty good at being myself!

~In Defense Of~

I would like to testify in defense of suffering and pain

I know many would disagree with me and instead they would complain

Pain does tend to be an intruder and suffering has robbed many of their quality of life

But in their defense they caused us to pray like never before

And at the same time, we learned how to remain steadfast and how to endure

So instead of condemning them for what they took us through

Let's just thank God that we came out stronger and much wiser too!

~God's Wonder~

A chilly high breezy wind on a hot summer day…

Blowing, seemingly out of nowhere

The sun beaming down on a frigid cold winter morning…

Oh, sweet wonder!

~Just A Matter of Time~

It's just a matter of time

Before you find the answers to all of the questions that are in your mind

And even those questions that you asked God and He chooses not to answer

It's just a matter of time that it will no longer matter!

~Beauty Secrets~

The process of obtaining and maintaining beauty is really overrated

You're told to do more of this and less of that

You're either too thin or much too fat

But the secret is right inside of you

Just be the best you, that's all you have to do

You see beauty is not something that you put on and take off

But it's a virtue obtained at a reasonable and affordable cost

You are a one-of-a-kind beauty that God designed

So share it with the world and let your beauty shine!

#Matthew 5:16

~*Everybody Has A Story*~

Everybody has a story

We all have something to tell

About all of the victories of life

And even about how many times we failed

It took the good, the bad, and the ugly

To make us what we are today

So please share your story with someone

As you pass along life's way

Your story helps me and mine helps you

We're better together and with each other's help
we'll make it through!

#Revelation 12:11

~Put It On~

Put it on and wear it well

You paid the price to be able to tell

That smile you're wearing, it cost a lot

You once didn't know whether you could afford it or not

And oh, the peace you have on, for it you got a great deal

What's so great about it is that it's paid in full, you don't have to receive a bill

As a matter of fact, Jesus purchased the whole outfit and paid the price for everything you own

All you had to do was accept it and put it on!

#Romans 13:4
#Ephesians 6:11

~What A Friend~

What is the purpose of a friend

Honestly, it's so many, I don't know where to begin

Really true friends come far and in between

But when you do find one, they will be there until the end

You may not talk to or see them every day

But you know that when you need them, they are not very far away

There are so many wonderful benefits of having a friend

But there is one that is the best part

No matter the circumstances, they forever remain in your heart!

#Dedicated to the memory of My Best Friend who is now with the Lord
#Pearl Williams

~Sing!~

Well, you may say singing is not my thing

But oh, you don't know what you are missing

For so much joy, it will surely bring

You don't need to take voice lessons or be accompanied by a band

Just OPEN UP your mouth, stomp your feet, and clap your two hands!

"Ya Betta Sang!!!"

~What Time Is It?~

What time is it, you may ask

My answer to you is, don't you know

It's time for you to walk through that door

What door is that, you're wondering my friend

It's the door that's been open for a while called Opportunity

But let me warn you that time is just about up

If you don't act quickly, the Door of Opportunity will soon be shut

And you will certainly regret it my friend

For you may not have that same Opportunity ever again

Because God is the one that opens those doors for you and me

So that we can fulfill our Purpose and Destiny!

~After~

Before you throw in the towel

Before you go backwards

Before you cave in

Before you give up again

Remember Before you do any of this

That AFTER comes with something that you don't want to miss!

~New Normals~

New normals are like receiving presents

You never know what to expect

But once you open them up

You'll find a wonderful surprise that is actually really great!

~Love Wins~

Love is a sore loser

He loves to win

That is why he just keeps on loving to the very end!

#I Corinthians 13:3-8
#Charity is Love

~It's Lonely Being Right~

If you ever get caught up in doing something wrong

You won't have any trouble finding someone to join you and come along

But when you make up your mind that you're going to do what's right

Sometimes everyone will scatter and it won't be a single person in sight!

~A Guilt Trip~

Don't allow the devil to take you on a guilt trip

Just because you may have made a mistake and slipped

Don't give Satan the wheel of your life to take you for a ride

He'll only drive you crazy and have you all messed up inside

He only wants to take you around in circles

Filling your head with first one thing and then another

Please don't let him take you there

It's just a trip that will take you NOWHERE!

~I'm Satisfied~

There was once a time in my life that I had to learn that no matter what was going on

I needed to be content

I didn't really understand how or why or the real reason for this

But then I began to understand what God meant and His word came alive

I realized that I needed to become content before I could become satisfied

I learned that being content is about waiting patiently on God to do what He wants to do

And when He finishes, you will be so satisfied that you will know just what to do!

~The Right Kind Of Love~

The right Kind of Love

Is the kind that I want my heart to be full of

The kind that protects me from all that is wrong

The kind that when I am weak

It continues loving and loving until I am strong

This is really the way LOVE should be

The kind that made Jesus die on calvary!

#St. John 3:16

~The Sun and The Moon~

The Sun and The Moon were both created by God

Ever since the beginning they both have been doing their job

To make this world a much better place to be

I think on this we both can agree

So you and I should be more like the Sun and the Moon

And be faithfully doing what we were created to do

Before The Sun goes down forever and The Moon drifts away!

#Psalms 104:19

~Fight The Right Thing~

There are times in this life that we fight to live

Trying so very hard not to give up and die

Then there are times when we find ourselves
fighting back the tears

So others won't see us cry

But there are rules in this life's fight

So just remember this

We don't fight against flesh and blood

And Thanks Be To God, the fight is fixed!

~Lost In The Desert~

I've never been lost in an actual desert

But I've experienced deserts of other kinds

As I look back over my life

One in particular comes to mind

I was lost in an emotional desert

While there I felt so all alone and isolated

I was extremely thirsty for an oasis of love

What I thought was it, was only a mirage, a place that left me dry

The only relief I had was from the tears that I often cried

It took me a while, but I found another route

By learning to love myself more was the best and only way out!

~Doors of Heaven~

The doors of Heaven are always open

Because the Angels of God are always coming and going

God is always sending them out

To make sure that His children are alright

So when we get to Heaven

We can walk right on in

Because the doors will be open and a sign saying WELCOME!

~Loving The Unlovely~

Loving the unlovely is showing love indeed

Because that is truly what they need

So don't be turned off by someone who is mean

Just keep right on loving them!
#Give a hug!

~In This Place~

For a very long time I was on a journey

Without knowing exactly to where

The route was very stressful and it was taking me

A long time to get there

So I began to really seek the Lord

About this tedious race

And He spoke back and said

"Where I'm taking you is not for the swift or the strong but you will get there by my grace"

So I picked myself up and continued on in haste

I'm here to tell you it was worth all I went through

To end up In This Place!

~I Am Rich~

Oh my, I'm filthy rich

No, I'm not talking about dollars and cents

But I have an abundance of peace and love

Sent down from my Heavenly Father up above

I have more than enough with yet room to spare

I believe I will find someone with whom I can share!

~God Said~

God said to me, "I saw you the day you were born"

He said, "I saw and knew all the times that you felt so all alone"

He said, "I had plans for you and knew your end from the beginning"

And He said, "And I was right there even in the middle!"

~Curl Up With The GOOD BOOK~

You need to take more time and curl up with the GOOD BOOK

Open it up and take a very close look

You will be so amazed at how it will make you feel

It will be as if the words jump off the pages and become so real

Yes eyes have not seen and ears have not heard

But you can Read All About It in THE GOOD BOOK called the BIBLE!

#Yes that's the book for me!

~Walking In God's Favor~

Walking in God's Favor is a blessing all by itself

It is God doing for you things that won't come from anyone else

He will open doors for you that no one can shut

That is why I love walking in God's Favor

It makes things so much easier!

~Loved Me To Life~

I once felt as if my very breath was being taken away

There was a time I didn't think that I would live to see this very day

I emotionally and mentally passed out from all the misery and strife

Then God resuscitated me by loving me back to life!

~Fill In The Blanks~

There was a time in my life that I asked the Lord, "Where do I go from here," after a season of going through

He answered me back and said, "It's entirely up to you"

He said, "For I have already provided you with everything that you need in the book of life"

"And there you will find everything laid out in stages"

"And as you trust and obey me, you will fill in the blank spaces!"

#True Story

~ *What If And Why Not?* ~

What If you missed your destiny

Because you got tired of staying on your knees

What If you failed to fulfill your purpose

Because you no longer wanted to suffer

What If God was to step back from us

Like we draw back from Him

That would be a life most miserable

Like never waking up from a bad dream

So Why Not submit to God's plan and will for you

Knowing that He will bring you out of whatever He takes you through!

~Gallon In A Pint~

My life is full of joy and peace

I'm just bubbling over thinking about the Goodness of Jesus and all that He's done for me

It would take the rest of my life to try and tell it all

So I'll just have to give you a little at a time

And try to put this "gallon in a pint"!

~Don't Get It Twisted~

Please don't get it twisted

If you do, it will be hard to untangle and fix it

Don't think of yourself more highly than you ought

If it had not been for the Lord on your side

You wouldn't be where you are

So stop running around trying to take His Glory

If it wasn't for Him, you would have an entirely different story!

#To God Be The Glory!

~God Specializes~

If you are searching for a specialist for a particular need

Why don't you try Jesus

I'm sure you will be absolutely pleased

He comes Highly Recommended for cases that are considered impossible

His Record exceeds that of any other doctor!

#HE IS THE HEALER

~God Is Fair~

Some people accuse God of not being fair

They just don't have a clue of how much He really cares

That's because His ways are not like ours, neither are His thoughts

We see only the outside of things and people

But God knows the heart!

#Isaiah 55:8-9

~Can You See Me Now~

Hey there, remember me

I know, I do look so much differently

I can hardly believe it myself

Since the last time you saw me

I've been extremely blessed

You remember me when, but look at me now

God turned things in my life completely around!

~Desperate Measures~

How bad do you want it

How far are you willing to go

These are just a few of the things

That our Lord and Savior wants to know

What are you willing to give up

To fulfill His Purpose for you

What are you willing to sacrifice

How much will you take while going through

Are you really desperate to reach your destiny

No matter how long it takes

Will you continue faithfully!!

~From A Dark Place To A Place of Healing~

Sometimes life can be like stumbling in the dark

You're not sure exactly where you're going

And seems like you're always missing the mark

But don't be afraid, for these times only last for a season

And believe me, our God knows and He allows it for a reason

If we never went through times of darkness

We wouldn't really appreciate the light

If we never had a battle

We would never learn how to fight

So never fear the darkness and how it leaves you feeling

It's only preparing you to appreciate that place of healing!

~Getting Better~

Better comes between Good and Best

It is the bridge that helps us cross and pass life tests

Good is only temporary and the Best is yet to come

But when things are Getting Better

You know that you've just overcome!

~Reign Over Pain~

One day I asked the Lord…

"If pain is a slave and we are its master

Why do we always become captive to pain's disaster"

Then one day the Lord responded to my cry

He said, "I know it's been a delay to your prayers but my child, it's not a denial

You see sometimes it's best for you that I don't immediately take away the pain

But instead I will teach you how to reign over it and that way there will be much more

Blessings for you to gain!"

~Loneliness And Unhappiness~

Loneliness and Unhappiness are not a match made in Heaven

It is only a temporary solution to hearts that are aching

If you look for love in all the wrong places

You will end up somewhere still lonely and un-happy!

~Where Do We Go~

Where do I go from here?

Is a question often asked

The answers are as many as the people who ask them

But from my experiences in life, I have learned to answer this question with a question

I ask myself

Where have you come from and where have you been

Then I ask myself

Do I want to go there again?!

~A Diamond In The Rough~

I don't mind starting off as a diamond in the rough

Because what it takes to make me shine will also make me tough!

#Bling! Bling!

~In Love With Sadness~

There was once a time when I thought I was in love with Sadness

He was always there and seemed to never leave me

When joy and happiness were nowhere to be found

Sadness was always hanging around

Even though he never gave me anything to be happy for

I didn't have the strength to put him out the door

Until one day I decided that I was tired of this relationship

So I broke it off and called it quits

That was one of the best decisions that I ever made

I'm in love with Joy now and we're enjoying happier days!

~I Couldn't Care Less~

I couldn't care less about life's disappointments
and let downs

Because there were much better opportunities
that finally came around

I couldn't care less about all the times I tried but
didn't succeed

Because it ended up being a blessing in disguise
that truly met the need

I couldn't care less about all the so called friends
that walked away

Because it only made room for the true friends
that decided to stay!

~Never Too Old~

You're never too old

To make a difference

You're never too old

To walk in a new season

You're never too old to begin again

Instead of just sitting around talking about

"I remember when"

You're never too old for a second chance

To ask life, "May I have the next dance?"!

~Only Believe~

Believing has a way of making things happen all
on his own

He doesn't need any doubters tagging along

You see he walks by faith and not by sight

He just believes that all things are possible and
somehow will turn out alright!

~Used By God~

I hope you know what you're in for when you ask
to be used by God

For it's about truly giving and making Him your
all and all

To be used by Him is not an impossibility

But it is all about your availability

When you say YES to Him, your life will surely change

What you know as life today will most certainly not remain the same!

~An Earthen Bank~

I want to be an earthen bank for my Lord

One that He can trust to deposit His Word

And when the time comes for Him to make a withdrawal

I will say, "Here am I Lord,

To you I will always be trustworthy and loyal"

I Invest all that you have given to me to use on this earth

To share with others The Eternal Security of the New Birth

And I vow that when the enemy comes in like a flood to rob this earthen bank

That I will guard and protect it with my life and soul and will never ever faint!

~Miracles Found In Misery~

Once life to me was such misery

I cried and I cried continually

I almost lost my ability to smile

Because of the awful pain that I felt inside

Seems like so much of what I needed was missing

There were times when I had no one to talk to or anybody who would even listen

Joy was gone so long that I forgot what it felt like

Seems as though it disappeared and was nowhere in sight

But after suffering what seemed like forever

I began to see a light at the end of the tunnel that made me feel better

As the Light got closer, I realized that it was my Lord and Savior, Jesus

He said I'm here to turn your misery into a MIR-ACLE!

~What In The World?~

What in this world do we expect to find?

Is it all about wealth and riches, or is it peace of mind?

What is it that we look for from day to day?

Is it just another paycheck or do we pray for hate and conflict to go away?

What in the world is holding Jesus from soon coming back?

IT IS all of the souls that are yet lost…

…And that my friend is a fact!

~The Voice Of The Lord~

The voice of the Lord can be large or small

Or it can actually be heard without any words at all

Sometimes the words from His voice can be so sweet

It just makes you want to melt and kneel down at His feet

Then there are times when the words He speaks are so stern

They cause you to get in a hurry and from your sins turn

Whatever tone of voice my Lord chooses to speak

You better respond and do it quick!

#Psalms 29:3-9

~Everything Won't Be The Same~

If everything in life that we experience is always exactly the same

Then we would absolutely not learn anything

For each and every thing that we go through teaches us a lesson

So the more we know, the more we grow and that in itself is truly a blessing!

~Almost~

Almost there can be anywhere

It all depends on where you are and where you are trying to go

Almost real is only a temporary thrill

But it is not a permanent deal

Almost finished is just an excuse to not stick with it

So don't settle for Almost

Because it is the enemy of endurance and completion!

~It May Just Be~

It may just be something that I really desire

Or it may be something that God requires

Whether it's something that God has planned

Or something completely out of my hands

It May Just Be just what I need!

104

~A Brand New Yes!~

I want to give God something new from me every day

Even though for all He's done for me, I could never repay

If I had a billion dollars that couldn't even begin to fit the bill

For all of the times that He healed my body and mind when I was very ill

I try to thank Him every day

When I kneel down to pray

Sometimes I become so overwhelmed with His love that I can hardly find the words to say

So I asked the Lord, what shall I render unto you for all that you do

And He answered, "If you really want to give me your best

Every day just give me a Brand New YES!"

#YES LORD!

~Friends~

Friends are like jigsaw puzzles

It takes each one to make your life complete

That is why it's no coincidence that you

Befriend those that you meet!

~Just Because~

Just because you tried and failed

Does not mean that you won't prevail

Just because you didn't succeed the first time

Doesn't mean it will be the same way the second
time around

Just because you're in an uncomfortable place
today

Does not mean that this is where you will always
stay

So, Just Because you faithfully struggled through

God has an amazing Just Because Blessing prepared just for you!

~Human Art!~

Human Art is a live, walking, talking, breathing, in living color Masterpiece

It's you and me and the entire race of God's created Family

We're all shapes, sizes, and colors that are so beautifully and uniquely designed

A universe museum full of art that is all one of a kind

So let every day be Human Art Appreciation Day as we value one another

Because it takes all of us to make a Rainbow of Colors!

~Talk To God More~

When we have a problem, we tend to talk to everyone we know

Only to end up more confused and not knowing which way to go

If we could just learn not to listen to all of the so and so

Instead realize that we would be better off if we talk to God more!

~Me~

There is a person that I live with each and every day

I'm very confident that they will never go away

This person is someone that I can always talk to when no one else is around

I can truly count on them to lift me up whenever I feel down

I really love this person so very dearly

You see this person just happens to be ME!

#I love myself some me
#Mirron Elaine

~Nothing Wasted!~

God talks to me sometimes

About the things that He allowed me to experience throughout my life

I must admit that I've had many questions

Concerning all of the things that had crushed me

He explained to me that He's always had plans to prosper me and not to harm me

And that sometimes those plans included hardships

Then He reassured me that even though some of what I went through was extremely painful

That He loved me through it all and that Nothing Was Wasted!

~Help Someone~

Help someone while you are going through

By allowing God to do all that He wants to do in you

Someone needs to be able to show others

Just how good God is when you are in the midst of your troubles

So help a brother or sister out

Don't wait til the battle is over, SHOUT NOW!!!

~I Want To~

I want to grow closer to my Lord every day

I want to be able to one day to hear Him say

"Well done, my good and faithful servant

Come on in, the Door Is Open!"

~Title Unknown…~

Never give a man or woman complete control of your life

God is the only one that has this right

So give all of you to Him as a living sacrifice

You will be much better off if you take this advice!

#Title Unknown…
#Avoid abuse of any kind

~No Turning Back~

As the hands on a clock continuously move forward

So should you keep your eyes fixed on what's in front of you

If you turn back, to what are you going?

To the same old, same old, that kept you complaining and groaning

Why would you want to again live like that

Please don't even think about turning back!

~I've Done Nothing Wrong~

I've done nothing wrong by deciding to move on

It ended up being the best decision of my life

Every time I think about it, it causes me to SMILE!!

~The Story Never Ends~

Your life's story will never end

There will only be new chapters over and over again

So live life to the fullest while you have a chance

And make your life's story the best that someone has ever read!

~I Will Never Forget~

I will never forget

The day that my purpose and destiny met

At first my purpose was going one way and my destiny another

Until I realized that they needed to meet each other

So God set it up where the three of us could meet

And ever since that day we've been a team that can't be beat!

~Power In Letting Go~

You ever wonder why it seems as though you're stuck

Seems like your life is in a rut

You've become mentally and emotionally drained

Can't accomplish anything without a struggle and strain

Well, I'm here to tell you what you probably already know

You will get your strength and zest back

When you finally realize there is POWER In Letting Go!

#stop holding on to what is holding you

~Going Pass The Obstacles~

When you're in life's obstacles course

Set your mind on finishing and just continue to go

Go pass all the roadblocks that try to entangle you

And eventually you will make it through

You see the main objective is to keep right on moving

Continue to go pass every obstacle that tries to hinder your endurance!

~To Be Continued~

I asked God a question

Where do I go from here?

You've brought me through so much

Up to the front of the line from being in the rear

Blessings and more blessings are overtaking me

He answered me, "To Be Continued, Just Wait Patiently and See!"

~Especially Yours~

God has some blessings that are being designed

As He is putting them together

He has You especially in mind

Are you ready because He's about to Open Heaven's Doors

And present to you something awesome, marked Especially Yours!

~Never A Boring Moment~

It seems as though there is always some heartaches and pains

I'm forever trying very hard not to complain

There is always a lot going on in this life as we are going through

But one thing that is very sure

There is never a boring moment!

~My Friend, Worse~

The worse thing that ever happened to you can be a foe or a friend

It's all in how you look at it

It just really depends

If you press through and pass life's test

That worse thing can become your friend and teach you what's really best

But if you mess around and fail to stay the course

Then you have made an enemy by the name of worse!

~In It To Win It~

Moment by moment, minute by minute

So close yet not quite at the finish

Throwing in the towel is not an option

But I've got to remain focused and proceed with caution

The race is not given to the swift

But to those who are in it to win it!

~Hot and Bothered~

There is a place called Hot and Bothered

I bet you know what I'm about to say

I'm sure it already sounds like somewhere you don't want to go

And surely don't want to stay

The saddest thing about this place is,

Once you're there, from there, there is no returning

No matter how hot and bothered you are,

For eternity you just keep right on burning

Yes, my friend this place is in Hell

You will be hot from the fire and bothered by the smoke

Believe me when I tell you, this place is really real and certainly is no joke!

#I ain't joking, hell is smoking
#Repent before it's too late

~Don't Pay For What You Didn't Purchase~

The Bible tells us that "man born of a woman, is a few days and full of trouble"

Today I would say, if it ain't one thing it's another

So don't go around looking for and shopping for more trouble

Don't make much sense to pay for something that you didn't even purchase!

~Won't God Do It~

Won't He do it each and every time

He'll open up closed doors and leave stumbling blocks behind

He will make a way out of no way

The problems that you're facing will not be able to stay

Won't God do it – you just wait and see

Whatever IT is will soon no longer be!

#won't He do it

~Pay Attention!~

Pay attention to any and everything

You never know what life is about to bring

The very thing that you decide to ignore

Could be the very exact thing that you've been praying and looking for!

~Warning: Danger!~

God always sends a warning before there is danger

Whether it be a word, sign, an Angel or even a stranger

Our job is to heed the warning

And not to try and decide from whom or what we will hear the alarming!

~Fight To Live~

There are all kinds of battles in this life we will have to fight

No matter what kind it is, they're all designed to knock us out

But with God on our side, we will come out alive

For we fight to live again

Eternally with the Lord when the fight in this life comes to an end!

~Permanent Past~

Oftentimes we attempt to return

To the very same thing that caused us harm

We tend to quickly forget that some things were never meant to be

What's in the past should remain there permanently!

~Coming Out Alive!~

"Stick'em up" screamed life's heartaches and pains

I'm here to rob you of all of your life, health, and strength

I thought about giving in because life had just about gotten the best of me

But then I remembered that this was the very same enemy

He had tried this very same thing before

Until I decided I wasn't going to take it any more

After a moment of reflecting and thinking for a while

I overcame that enemy and with the help of God, once again, I came out alive!

~From The Desert To The River~

Some seasons of your life are like a journey in a desert

Things are extremely hot and dry

There's not even a sign of rain in the sky

My brothers and sisters, the struggle is real

Trust me, I now exactly how you feel

But if you cry out to God, he will bring you out and deliver

Before you know it, you will go from the desert to the river!

#Exodus 23:31
#Psalms 105:41

~Get To Stepping~

Step by step life's journey can be

Even when what's right in front of you, you can hardly see

Just by faith, take one step at a time

With prayer and determination, your purpose and destiny you will soon find!

#II Corinthians 5:7

~Make The Most Of It~

Take those heartaches and pains

Ask God to give you more strength and tolerance

So that you can make the most of it

When your spirit and mind feel really really ill

Instead of taking another pill

Leap for joy and make the most of it

Everything happens for a purpose

But God designed it that way so that we may grow and endure to the end

So instead of always trying to find the easy way out

Just make the most of it my friend!

~Pay Attention~

Pay attention to God's still small voice

That urges you to make a choice

Pay close attention to the Cross ✠

Where our Savior hung upon to save the lost

Please pay attention to the signs and warnings

That say that Jesus will be soon returning!

#Pay Attention or Pay Later
#Romans 6:23

~It's A Gift, Receive It~

The Gift of Salvation is free, receive it

It is so priceless and precious that people can hardly believe it

It's wrapped with a red bow of Jesus' Blood that He shed for us

To get into Heaven, receiving it is a must!

~Great Expectations~

Great expectations sharpen your faith

Don't ever doubt it, make no mistake

"Faith is the substance of things hoped for, the evidence of things not seen"

Great expectations keep you holding on and believing to the very end!

~Spring Cleaning~

God has opened up the windows of Heaven for spring cleaning

So much He's pouring out to those who have been faithfully giving

When He's done you won't have room to receive

Blessings are springing forward to all who believe!
#Malachi 3:10

~It Was Worth It~

It was worth everything that I went through

To be able to share my story with you

I didn't feel that way then

But if I had to I would do it all over again

If it will make things easier in life for you

It was worth all I had to endure

I truly paid a price to be where I am today

But it was worth it, if it will help you to prevail!

~Open Doors~

An open door is what we often strive for!

Life can shut so many doors in our face

That causes us to become discouraged in this race

But when that season of closed doors is up

God will open doors that no one can shut!

~I'm Not Afraid~

I'm no longer afraid of the unknown

That is why I just keep on dancing and singing a song

I'm not afraid anymore of how long a test will take

For I have learned that good things come to those who patiently wait

I'm so glad I'm not afraid of what people think of me

Because my God is the only one that I want to please!

~Learning To Lose~

Ask God to help you to forget where you have the hurt

And tell your heart to no longer continue to search

For all of the things that caused you pain

There's no need to rehearse it over and over again

He will teach you how to delete it from your mind

It will become lost and no longer to be found!

~Fight~

Fight temptation and its attempt to overtake you

Fight oppressions in your soul

That try to hinder you from becoming whole

Fight back everything that is fighting you

God is on your side and with Him, all things you can do

For Greater is He, than he that is in the world

The Fight is fixed, so REJOICE!

#Psalms 35:1-9

~You Just Never Know~

Oftentimes we just never know the reason or the purpose

For the course that our lives will take

Or for the good times and even all of the mistakes

But we can rest assure that God works them all in His plans for you and me

And when He has finished, it's called our DESTINY!

~I'm Here To Tell You~

I went through some things that nearly took me out

I was like, "Ummmm…What in the world was that all about?"

But God helped me to get back up on my feet

Not realizing that there were more trials and tests that I would run into and meet

Once again God gave me His Grace to make it through

So He left me here so that I could tell you!

~I'm Full~

I'm full up to and over my head

Of all the negative things that I've heard said

About life being so hard

And yes, it can be if you try to live it without the Lord

I thirst and hunger the more for Him each and every day

Lord "fill me up" is what I pray!

#Philippians 4:18-19

~Hook-Up or Hiccups~

Our lives cross the paths of so many people as we pass this way

With some that we meet, it's an instant connect

Then there are others, after a while, we wish we had never met

With some we are able to hook-up,

Become good friends and so much from them we can learn

Then there are others with whom we would like

To just turn away from and run

Some people we meet are like the hiccups

They make us feel bad and seem like will never go away

But whether it's a hook-up or a hiccup,

You will run into your share in this life's race!

~From Fear To Hope~

There was once a time in my life that I battled with fear

There was always a problem that out of nowhere would appear

Things were coming at me so fast

I would often wonder, how long will this last

Then God would often remind me that He hadn't given me the "spirit of fear"

I had nothing to worry about because He was always near

Then when it seemed like I could no longer cope

I let go of the fear and grabbed hold of hope!

~A Place Without Walls~

There is a place without walls

If you end up there you will do nothing but continue to fall

For this place is a bottomless pit

You will burn and burn and never ever quit

Please believe me you don't want to go there

Just the thought of it, I can hardly bear

But there is another place without walls

It is the most Glorious place of them all

I hear that the streets are paved with gold

I believe that the half has not even been told

Now this place without walls I truly long to see

Because it surely does sound like HEAVEN to me!

~Tomorrow Will Be Better~

Tomorrow will be better than it is today

Things have a way of getting better, and sooner or later will go away

Things will be better tomorrow

You just wait and see

Just as sure as there's a problem

There is a remedy

Every day has its own circumstances, heartaches, and pains that we must endure

But trust me, tomorrow will be better and will bring with it a cure!

~A Homeless Heart~

A homeless heart is a lonely heart that roams
from place to place

It has been searching desperately for a permanent
place to stay

It has been evicted countless times from broken
relationships

It was unable to function for a while when in-love
it fell and then later slipped

But now it's beginning to pump and beat again

Because it finally found true love that was glad to
take it in!

~Do You!~

Before you die, you should do what you were
born to do

If you yet don't know what it is

It's time, my friend for you to make sure

You were not born to just take up some space

But to be busy, occupying your God-given place

Remember life is short and death is sure

Someone and the world is waiting for you to

Do You!

#Luke 19:13

~I Can't Stand~

I can't stand the thought of ever going back

To the place that was once my old familiar habitat

I can't help but think that I stayed there much too long

Because it had become my comfort zone so I called it home

I thought that from there, I would never leave

But I had only myself to blame for being so deceived

Now I can't stand around wasting any more time

I'm moving on with my life!

~Chain Reaction~

Seems like it's always one thing after another

Nothing but trouble on top of trouble

But then things will reverse and get better again

What you will end up with is an amazing chain reaction!

~Baby Steps~

Baby steps may be small

But they help us learn how to walk

To walk away from whatever that has you bound

They teach you how to get back up when you fall down

Baby steps teach you not only how to walk but also how to run

For in this life's race, the best is yet to come!

~The Body~

The body is an amazing machine

Unlike anything in this world that you have ever seen

It takes after its Creator and Maker

And for that we should be eternally grateful

That is why we should present our bodies to the Lord

And make Him The Lord and Savior of us all!

#Romans 12:1

~Never Mind~

Never mind what people around you say or think

Don't pay any attention to all the negativity

Instead keep your mind focused on God

And he will give you peace that you never thought was possible!

~A Makeover~

Are you in need of a makeover

But you don't know where to start

Just consult your Creator and Maker

And give Him complete charge of your heart!

#If any man be in Christ, he is a new creature…II Corinthians 5:17

~Get Up and Go Again~

Do you remember when

You were in a life's race and you were trying so hard to win

You got knocked down and were about to give in

But God said, "Oh no you don't, you're too close

Get Up and Go Again!"

~With Room To Spare~

My, oh my, just look a'there

How God has blessed me with room to spare

And oh wow, the blessings are about to overtake me

He's about to open up the windows of Heaven and pour me out a blessing

That I won't have room to receive!

#you can't beat God giving

~I Feel Good~

I feel so good about what God has brought me through

I thank Him so much for what He's done and what He is going to do

When I look back and see where He's brought me from

I feel so good

It makes me want to leap and dance and break out in a song!

#I feel GOOD

~Harvest Time~

Jesus said the Harvest is plenteous

But the workers are few

That means that we need to get busy

Because there is plenty to do

Because Jesus, Our Lord and Savior, is soon to come

It's time to make sure that His work is getting done!

~I'll Take You There~

God said to me, "I'll take you there

To that place that I've prepared for you

When you had all that you can bear"

He said, "I will pick you up and carry you over

All of your trials, tribulations, and troubles

So cast all of your cares", He said, "unto me

And it will be so easy, you just wait and see!"

#Matthew 11:28-30

~Jesus Really Loves Me~

Jesus really loves me

He's proved it over and over again

He even gave His life for me when I was drowning in my sins

So there is nothing else that He has to do

To prove to me that His love is really true!

~The Will of God~

The will of God can be somewhat a mystery

But one thing for sure is if you stay on your knees

And seek His Face and not always His Hand

He will begin to reveal to you some of His Plans!

~God Is In Control~

God is yet in control

His might and power is so amazing to behold

Even though there's a lot going on in this world

There is still nothing that He is not aware of

So don't fool yourself

He knows and He sees

And when the time comes, He will supply every need!

~Ain't Nobody Mad But The Devil~

Ain't nobody mad but the devil

He can't believe that you made it past him and went to the next level

He's so mad, he's just about had a stroke

Overcoming that ole devil, ain't no joke!

#Make the devil mad
#I John 4:4

~Bitter Words~

Please beware of bitter words

Spoken from you or to you

That are best left unheard

Instead feed yourself on words that are sweet

It makes for a much better feast!

~Count Your Blessings~

Can you count your blessings

Can you remember each and every one

You could try your very best

But I am sure that you would forget some

If you are anything like me, there are so very many

It's almost impossible to count them and not leave out any

So when you try to count your blessings

It's a blessing when you realize that your blessings are countless!

~Only One Moment~

Only one moment between life and death

Only one moment before you could take that last breath

Only one moment it could be before Jesus comes back

In that one moment you could be left and that's a fact

#St. Luke 12:40
#I Corinthians 15:52

~Out of Your Misery~

How did you get to a place of misery

It seems like you got there overnight but it just can't be

For things go from bad to worse over time

Before you became miserable you were doing just fine

143

But there is a way out of this misery

Give it to God, and go to sleep

And I declare to you that when you awake you will feel much better

Now stay out of misery and get yourself together!

~Why Am I Poor~

hy Am I poor in Joy

When there is so much to be excited for

Why Am I poor in Love

When I know the ONE who can send it from above

Why Am I poor in Faith

When all I have to do is believe and claim it

Why Am I now poor in tears?

Because I have overcome everything that I once feared!

#Psalms 70:5
#Matthew 3:5

~More and More~

I realize more and more that there is much to thank God for

With the passing of each and every day

I realize that there is so much I want to say

Because He keeps on doing great things for me

So more and more, I want to PRAISE HIM continually!

#Psalms 71:14

~Take Off The Lamp Shade~

We are like lamps for God shining with His light

That is why it is important to always do that which is right

Because when we don't our light will begin to fade

Then it's time my sister and brother to take off that lamp shade!

#Matthew 5:14-16

~How To Live Forever~

How do you live forever? That's a good question.

I'm so glad that you asked!

Just give your life totally to Jesus!

He promised in His Word and He cannot lie

Once you leave this world and go to be with Him

You will live forever and never again will you die!

~My Life Is Over~

I had all the plans for my life together

At least that's what I thought

Until all my plans went upside down and came to a complete halt

So I figured that life for me was all over

It was just too much damage for me to try and recover

Then Jesus offered me a brand new life in Him

And now I've been living for Him abundantly!

~A Turn For The Better~

Once my life was headed for the worse

No matter how hard I tried it wouldn't change its course

Then one day God spoke to me

And said, "Why don't you try it my way and see"

He said, "My ways are not your ways, neither are my thoughts your thoughts"

So in the middle of nowhere I came to a complete stop

Ever since I followed His map and directions

My life has taken a complete turn for the better!

~First Responder~

Don't be so quick to respond to harsh words that are spoken to you

Take this advice, this what you should do

Be quick to hear and slow to speak

Let this be your first responder and keep your

tongue between your cheeks!

#Sometimes no response is the best response
#Take a deep breath…
#Let silence be your first responder

~A Quiet Place~

A Quiet Place is like Heaven here on earth

A place where you have a moment of not being interrupted or disturbed

But one day we will forever be with God there

At that eternal quiet place that He has prepared!

~The Days of Our Lives~

The days of our lives are filled with so many surprises

We never know from one day to the next

Just what is going to happen and what to expect

But one thing is sure, God is always in control

No matter what the days of our lives will unfold!

~Beat Down~

The "ole" devil knocked me down but didn't
knock me out

I was down to almost the count of ten

But by the Grace of God I got up again

I told the referee I demand a rematch

Because that ole devil doesn't fight fair

So I was given another round

And ended up giving that ole devil the beat
down!

#Psalms 89:22-23

~You're In Good Hands~

Why are you so full of fear

God didn't give it to you plus He's always near

Why are you so anxious about everything

God doesn't want you to worry about tomorrow
or what it could bring

149

"In His Right Hand, there are pleasures for evermore!"

So remember you're in Good Hands

So chill out, relax, and enjoy the overflow!

#Psalms 16:5-11

~Wipe That Grin OFF the Devil's Face~

You want to know how to wipe that grin off the devil's face

Just cry out to God, asking Him for more strength and grace

In an instant the devil will become so nervous

And that grin will melt off his face in a hurry!

~A Reason For The Season~

There is a reason for each season that we go through in life

Whether it seem like it's lasting forever or for a very short time

Just remember God has a purpose for everything that we go through

If He brings us to it, he will take us through it, that is for sure!

~God Remembers~

God remembers when others forget

And He has blessings for you that you have not received yet

So don't think for a moment that He has forgotten you

Because you're always on His mind and of that you can be sure!

~A Rainy Day~

A rainy day is about more than God pouring water from the sky

It is about going through seasons of situations that cause you to wonder why

Why this and why that

A rainy day can be perplexing and that is a fact

But if you want those rainy days to pass quickly away

Instead of complaining, just learn how to pray

#Rain Rain Go Away
#Pray Pray Pray!

~Unwanted Visitors~

There is always an unwanted visitor knocking at my door of life

Heartaches and pain have showed up more than once or twice

I have told them over and over that they can't come in

But they keep right on coming and knocking again and again

They keep talking about that they need somewhere to hang out

I told them, oh no, it won't be here

My faith is stronger now, I trust God and He has removed all doubt

You see I'm healed now, you have to find somewhere else to stay

You're no longer welcome, so just go on your way!

~Hell Is Real!~

Hell Is Real Y'all

You don't have to go in order to know

That it's a real place

And it continues to enlarge its space

So give your life to Christ before it's too late

If you don't, it will be your biggest and eternal mistake!

~The Devil Didn't Know Who He Was Messing With~

Satan didn't know who he was messing with

When he tried to deceive me with his same old tricks

He thought by now I would've surely failed

And he would drag me down with him back into hell

But instead I pleaded the BLOOD OF JESUS against him and sent him back to his pit

And that's where he is now having a devilish fit!

~When God Says It's Time~

When God says, "It's time"

No one or anything can interfere

When you hear these words spoken by Him

Some amazing blessings are about to appear

The kind of blessings that will absolutely blow your mind

Will come to pass whenever God says

"It's Time!"

~Don't Forget~

Don't forget that God is not through blessing you yet

He has more on His Things To Do List for you

For all that you have gone through

So continue to finish faithfully every test

And don't forget to do your best!

~Just Do It~

Just do whatever it is that God has for you to do

He's already told you and showed you too

So why are you yet slowing around

The end is closer than you think and time is running out!

~Don't Stay Where You Started~

Don't stay in your mind where you started

You need to take and renew your mind once your body has departed

Beware of mentally continuing to stay

At the place where God has taken you away!

~A Healed Wound~

When a wound is healed

You will be able to tell by the way you feel

There won't be any emotional pain from the past

No regrets, no setbacks, none of that will last!

~Let Me See~

Oh my goodness, let me see

Could this possibly be

God has completely turned things around for me

I can actually see a brighter day

All kinds of blessings are coming my way

Keep walking by faith and not by sight

You will see a breakthrough in a little while!

~Go Fishing~

There is a world of opportunities swimming in the sea of life

So why are you just sitting on the bank just watching them pass you by

They're not going to come to you by just watching and wishing

My friend it's time for you to go fishing!

~Can You See What I See~

Oh I wonder can you see what I see

Something that is about to happen

And it's not just my imagination

Jesus, our Lord and Savior, is so soon to return

Oh my God, it's sooner than you think

Are you ready, here He comes

In a moment, in a twinkling of the eye

My Lord and Savior will split the sky!

~Above My Head~

There is so much up above my head

That is why I choose to look up instead

Of focusing on what is on the ground

Or walking around with a frown

God's glorious sky full of stars and blue fluffy clouds

Are just some of the things that cause me to smile

That is why I set my affections on things above

Because that is where there's evidence that God is Love!

#Colossians3:2

~Color Me~

Color me a shade of gladness

After I've overcome a season of sadness

Color me a rainbow

The clouds of my life are in the past

I'm happy at last

Color me Deep BOLD RED

I'm covered by THE BLOOD OF JESUS!

~Love Seeds~

Love seeds do not grow as fast as weeds

It takes time to get to know

That special one that you love so

And as time goes by

You will understand and know why

It grows deeper and stronger until the day you die!

~Do You Hear What I Hear~

What is that I hear

It sounds like the rustling of someone about to appear

Wait, I think I hear it coming a little closer…

Did you hear that?!

#Jesus Is Soon To Come

~One Way Ticket~

If you could get a one-way ticket to anywhere in the world

To live forever as free as a bird

Where do you think that place would be

I don't know about you but I would choose to go where Jesus is Eternally!

~Power In Transitions~

There is so much power in going through life-changing transitions

A ton of life lessons are to be found in each and every mission

It's so amazing how strong you can become from going through things that are so hard

Truly this kind of strength and power can come only from the Lord!

~If God Said It~

If God said it, it will surely come to pass

It doesn't really matter whether it's slow or fast

All we have to do is never doubt

And in God's own good time

He will work it out!

~Take It Away~

There are some things that come into our lives
that don't need to stay

When they do we need to ask the Lord to take it
away

We were not created to be burdened down with
worry and despair

So learn to take them to the Lord and leave them
there!

~The Hurt Won't Hurt You~

When you are really hurting while going through

Let me tell you that the hurt doesn't have to hurt you

I know you may say that's easier said than done

But please hear the testimony of someone who has overcome

I was once hurting so bad that I thought it was more than I could bear

But God made a way of escape and seems like help came out of nowhere

So please believe when I say if He did it for me

He will take your hurt and make it disappear!

~Reading Between The Lines~

If you read between the lines

There is no telling what you may find

There is a lot being said without a whole lot of words

But instead,

Look beyond what you may actually see

What you won't find on pen and paper is

Written in the heart inwardly!

~Disturbed Peace~

What do you do when your peace is disturbed

When it seems like God is silent and there's no comforting words

Just keep your mind focused on the Lord

And sooner or later your peace will be restored!

#Isaiah 26:3

~In A Hurry To Worry~

Don't be in a hurry to worry

Trust me if you do, later on you will be sorry

Worrying does not solve anything

Just more trouble it seems to bring!

~I Don't Want To Go!~

I don't want to go to any place where God is not leading me

But I want to always be in His Perfect will continuously

I don't want to do anything on my own

But I want to know that He is right beside me and that I'm never alone

I don't want to go to Hell

Locked up forever in a burning, fiery jail cell!!!

~Blood and Love~

The blood that runs through our veins is like a river

It runs deep and wide throughout our entire life

It always flows back to the ones that we first learned to love

Even when those same ones hurt us

It doesn't change the blood

Once that love mixes with the blood

It will remain until death do you depart!

~It's What You Make It~

A little of this and a whole lot of that

Only God knows how much I can bear and how long it takes

So instead of adding too much grumbling and complaining

I think I'll make the most of it and put in some more praying and praising!

~Unforgiveness~

It's amazing how much harm we can bring to ourselves

When we refuse to forgive someone else

Yes, sometimes others will do us wrong

But we must never hold it against them too long

Unforgiveness will only hold you back

You will be the only one to suffer and that my friend is a fact

So take all your offenses to the Lord in prayer

And don't forget to leave them there!

#Forgive, Forget, and Move On
#Matthew 6:12-15

~Thankfulness~

Thankfulness is the key to open the door to more and more blessings

The more we thank God, the more He will do

An abundant harvest will overtake you!

~Statistics~

Statistics is just man's way of trying to keep record of what's going on in the world.

But what man has failed to realize is that God is still in control

And has been ever since He breathed into man's nostril and he became a living soul!

So even though man's record right now looks somewhat bleak

If you track God's Record, it always shows VIC-TORY!!!

~Success~

Success comes after you have tried your very best

Even though you didn't always pass every test

But in reality you achieved success because you didn't stop

For that's the only way to get from the bottom to the top!

~Passion~

When you have passion for something,

You have ignited a romance between your desires and your ambitions.

From that comes an emotional affair that surpasses

Any outside distractions or oppositions!

~Worrying~

Worrying is the disability of the spirit

Causing it not to function the way it was intended

So Don't Worry, just cast all your cares on the
Lord

Just BE Happy and allow Him to take charge!

~Vision~

Vision for your life is something that you should
cherish

For without it you will surely perish

Vision is the vehicle that takes you to your goals

It allows you to see it before you obtain it

Oh what a sight to behold!

~Truth~

If only more people would just speak the truth

But for some they just refuse to

It is not a language that's difficult to learn

The more you speak it, the better at it you will become!

~Resistance~

Resistance is a form of strength

Placed inside of us by God

It enables us to make the distance

When things get very hard

It causes us to ignore everything that tries to block our flow

The more that you resist whatever it is,

It will go away and bother you no more!

~JOY~

Sometimes joy is confused with happiness but there is a difference. Happiness is conditional but joy grows over time like a seed that is planted by a river of water. Eventually it becomes rooted and grounded so much that it is impossible to pluck up. As it continues to flourish, it produces fruit called strength!

#The Joy of the Lord planted grows strength

#Plant seeds of Joy and grow stronger and stronger

~Justice~

Don't get bent out of shape because someone does you wrong

"Vengeance is mine" saith the Lord and it won't be long

So don't spend a lot of energy worrying and fretting

When God gets through, it will be JUST as if it never happened!

~Strength~

Strength is an amazing virtue

It's created and designed by God for us to help lift up one another

When I am weak you are strong

When I am strong you may be weak

But we will both get what we need at our Savior's feet

When He gives you strength, it's not for you alone

But it's so that you can help me to carry on!

~Relief~

Relief can be spelled many different ways

It all depends on how much you appreciate the price that our Savior paid

You can spell it "S-A-V-E-D" or "H-E-A-L-E-D"

It really doesn't matter, Oh What a RELIEF it is!

~Dreamers~

A dreamer is not just someone who has s dream

But one who understands that it's important to find out what that dream means

They realize that once they awake from that dream

That the time that has passed, they must surely redeem

For once that time has been lost

It can only be bought back at a much higher cost

Dreamers don't just have dreams

But they spend time dreaming about making those dreams come true!

~Trust~

T – Totally

R – Relying

U – Upon

S – Someone's

T – Truthfulness

When you say that you trust someone

What does that really mean?

It should mean that you can rely on them to be totally truthful with you

Even when they are not being seen!

#Trust the Lord with all your heart
#Proverbs 3:5-8

~Disappointments~

Disappointments are missed appointments and opportunities to celebrate and to be happy about what you thought life had scheduled for you!

But don't be disheartened. You can always re-schedule if you don't allow it to get the best of you. The appointment has been postponed, not cancelled!

#II Corinthians 4:8-10

~Revenge~

Revenge can be a very dangerous thing

Attempting to go back and return harm to someone again

That's not the way God would have it to be

He said in His Word, "Just leave all of that to me"

He will take care of it, you just wait and see

Go on with your life and live peaceably!

#Deuteronomy 32:35
#Romans 12:18-21

~Time~

God gave us time so that we could see

That we can't take all day to do what is necessary

For one day with the Lord is as a thousand years

But according to the time clock that He gave us

It's later than it appears

So hurry up and stop wasting time

Once it's gone you won't be able to rewind!

#Ecclesiastes 3:1-8

~Today~

Today was yesterday

Tomorrow will be today

So don't get your days mixed up!

#Don't keep putting off today for tomorrow
#Psalms 95:7-8

~Worrying~

God never intended for us to be overly concerned

Especially about the things that He has already done

So why do we keep carrying around

Those things that do nothing but keep us bound

Worrying is like remaining in prison after you have been released

In order to be free my friend, the worrying must cease!

#Phillipians 4:4-7

~Comfort~

Comfort is the birth child of Peace and Rest. Peace and Rest are a match made in Heaven. They are both very affectionate toward each other so they couldn't help but to conceive and give birth to a child such as Comfort!

When you are around Comfort, you immediately feel the genetics that Comfort gets from both birth parents, Peace and Rest.

It is no doubt about it, Comfort is Peace and Rest's Love Child!

~Forgiveness~

When you forgive someone, you are giving God the opportunity to do what He really loves and wants to do for you! He loves to open up the windows of Heaven and pour you out a blessing!

You see when we forgive, we are releasing toxic waste that can cause us to become emotionally, spiritually, and even physically depleted!

So when we forgive and release, God gives us back more of what we need to heal, revive, and prosper!

~Courage~

Courage seems to get stronger and more bold as it ages

It just keeps on getting more and more courageous

It encourages everyone it meets

To stand up for what they believe in and never accept defeat

It makes you feel that there is nothing that you can't tackle

And gives you what you need to fight and win all of life's battles!

~Grace~

Grace is like putting medicine on a wound

In due time you will feel much better soon

God's Grace is sufficient when it's applied

When you think you can't make it

It helps you go that extra mile!

#God's Grace Is Sufficient
#II Corinthians 12:9

~Conflict~

Conflict will give you its hardest lick

But even though you may fall down, you must learn to get up quick

You see conflict is like a bully

Its bark is worse than its bite

Sometimes the solution to a conflict

Is to learn to stand up and fight for what is right!

~Strength~

Strength to endure another season of pressure!

Strength to remain calm when going through a storm!

Strength to yet dance no matter what happens!

Strength to tell God, Thank You, in the midst of going through!

Strength to Rejoice!

Because the Joy of the Lord IS My STRENGTH!

~Rejection~

Rejection is an emotional disease

It starts in the heart and soul of someone who desires desperately to please

Those who suffer with it, suppress their feelings deep down inside

This is the only way that they feel that they can survive

But if you are someone who this has happened to

I want you to know that God has not rejected you

He desires for you to be set free

Jesus is the Healer of all our diseases

He, Himself, was despised and rejected

So, he knows how you feel

He died on the cross so that you can be healed

#Psalms 103:1-3

~*Love*~

There was once something created called LOVE

It was made up in Heaven above

It was then sent down to the earth

In the form of Jesus Christ's birth

For God wanted the whole world to know

Just how much He Loved us so

And If we only believe in Him

We can have this LOVE Eternally!

#St. John 3:16

~Inspiration~

Inspirations are our stepping stones to our destination

Without them we would never arrive

For they boost us when we are discouraged

And they help us to continue to strive

Sometimes they come from people that we meet

Or something we happened to hear or see

But from whomever or whatever we become inspired

It's God's way of saying,

"Don't give up, just continue to thrive!"

~Family~

There are some very special people in this world that I have come to love and know

They will always be dear to my heart, no matter where in life I happen to go

Whether by blood or close familiarity

I call these special people my Family!

#Family group hug!!!

~Favor~

Tell me, how in the world did you get that job

You were underqualified and you don't even have a college diploma

And on top of that, you got promoted

If man had his way, you would have been out voted

All of this and more you received and didn't pay a dime for

Without a doubt, it ain't nothing but

God's Favor!

#Psalms 44:1-3

~Help~

Help can come in so many different ways

I can't begin to count them but just let me say

Help may not come when you want it

But God makes sure that it's right on time

Help that is sent by God is always the right kind!

#Psalms 46:1

~Tears~

Circumstances on the outside look one way

But it's not really how it appears

Just when you think you got it all hid

Here comes the tears

Tears will give you away every time

Whether it's joy, sorrow, or something that is pressing heavy on your mind!

#God understands our tears
#Psalms 56:8-9

~Rain~

Rain comes in many forms other than water pouring from the sky

It sometimes rains a flood of trouble that makes you wonder why

But one thing for sure that I have lived long enough to know

After the rain and flood, there is always a rainbow!

#Psalms 68:9

~Benefits~

Along with God's blessings comes many benefits

That is why I will always serve Him and never quit

Sometimes even the benefits far outweigh the blessings

The benefits come when I learn all the wonderful life lessons!

#Psalms 68:19
#Psalms 103:2
#Psalms 116:12

~Death~

We will experience many deaths before we die

Death of relationships, dreams, opportunities, and many more will pass us by

But it's not for us to stop and try to figure out why

But we must continue to live and not die!

#Psalms 118:17

~The Mind~

What are you thinking about most of the time

You know you can become whatever is on your mind

So make sure your thoughts are good

So that you will become the person that you should!

~Music~

Something about music, it's so pleasant and soothing to the ears

A universal language spoken more often than tears

It flows like a mighty river from the ears to the heart

Something so amazing could be created only by God

And oh, let's not forget what it does to the soul

Something even more precious than pure gold!

#"Up above my head I hear music in the air… there must be a God somewhere"

~Memories~

Memories are our constant companion

We carry them with us everywhere

So remember to make the best of each moment

So that your memories won't be hard to bear!

~Pride~

The Bible tells us that pride comes before a fall

But if you humble yourself, you can get back up with a fresh new start

But beware because pride is hard to hide

It can creep back in inwardly and eventually show up on the outside!

~Grief~

Healthy grief can bring you relief

From the loss that makes you sad

It's a process that takes longer for some than others

So don't let this make you feel bad

Allow God to minister to you directly

Or He may let it come through someone else

Just remember that you are not alone

So don't try to go through it by yourself!

~Oppression~

Oppression wants to make a bad impression on your spirit that is intended to last

But Jesus came to relieve you of it and make it a thing of the past

So allow Him to do what He came to do

And that is to set you free and make you a better you!

~Excellence~

Excellence is a virtue given to us from God

It causes us to do over and beyond what is required for any job

Whether you know it or not it's inside each of us

When you come across something that you are passionate about

You won't stop until it's excellent!

~Frustrations ~

Frustrations can work in your favor

They teach you how to become an overcomer without wavering

Their only purpose is to make you give up

But they can't stop you, they can only interrupt!

~Crying~

Oftentimes in this life we will find ourselves crying

But it's not always all about the tears

Sometimes we've been crying out to God asking Him

"Oh Lord, will you help me please"

Or it may be our hearts are crying out for love

Looking for it in all the wrong places

Instead of receiving it from the Father up above

Whatever the reason you are crying and whatever it's all about

Just continue to cry out to God and He will work it out!

~Faithfulness~

God is keeping record of your faithfulness

So when it's time for a promotion you will be next

He told you "if you be faithful over a few things that

He will make you ruler over many"

So get ready for your season of plenty!

~Jealousy~

Jealousy is like drinking poison that has been mixed in Kool-Aid. It may taste good to you but eventually it will kill you!

*#Don't kill yourself being jealous of someone else
#Jealousy is suicide*

~Interruptions~

God causes interruptions so that we can avoid all kinds of corruptions!

You see the enemy is always setting traps

But God always knows exactly where they're at

So He causes interruptions of what we have planned

So that we won't become prey to the enemy and fall into his hands!

~Influence~

We all have influence in this world

God calls it Light and Salt

So let your light so shine and be doers of all that Jesus has taught!

#Matthew 5:13-16

~Peace~

Peace is not only about external quiet and stillness

But about an internal rest free from all that can alarm us

This kind of peace surpasses all understanding and comes only from God

It is cradled deep down where no one can disturb it

Tucked away in the bed of our hearts!

#Philippians 4:7

~Longsuffering~

Longsuffering is not about suffering long

But it's about going through, enduring, and coming out strong!

~Desires~

Some things in life we want and others we desire

The things we want are necessary

But the desires we acquire

We want God to take away all of the trouble

But after He takes it away, we desire for Him to bless us double

But don't worry about it because He wants to give us the desire of our heart

But just remember that our ways must please
Him first!

~Life Changers~

What do we call those things that turn our life
upside down

That wipes the smile off our face and replaces it
with a frown

What do we call those things that keep us up
praying all night

Hoping it will be much better at the break of
daylight

We might call them heartaches, trouble, and
maybe even danger

But God has a plan, so He calls them Life-Chang-
ers!

~Complaining~

Why do we find it so easy to complain

If the sun is shining, we want it to rain

We're unhappy because it's either too cold or too hot

We ain't never satisfied with what we got

We need to take the time to look around us and see

That there's more to be thankful for than to be complaining!

~Chosen~

To be chosen by God should be very dear to your heart

Because few are chosen even though many are called

So don't take lightly this divine opportunity

Because one day you will have to answer to God for being chosen to represent Him!

~Sin~

Sin will take you places that you've never been

And will keep you there longer than you want to stay

So please don't play with sin

Ask God to cleanse you of all sin and do it right away!

#REPENT!

~Hesitation~

Hesitation is often mistaken for being patient

But in actuality they are not even related

Some people just use that as an excuse to put off doing what they are supposed to do

Patience even becomes so agitated waiting on Hesitation to get his act together!

~Be Nice~

It's just nice to be nice

And be a blessing to someone's life

Just a smile or a kind word is all it takes

But oh what a big difference it will make

So, if you haven't already, practice being nice

And experience a warm and fuzzy feeling inside!

~Scar Tissue~

Scar tissue is a result of unresolved heart issues

They form from learning how to perform

Over things that have us damaged and caused us great harm

But God wants to remove all of the scars

That we have tried to cover up in our hearts

So allow Him to take all the scar tissue away

Don't continue to be deceived, do it without delay!

#Jermiah 17:9, 10

~Diseases~

Diseases make us uneasy

And there are many kinds

It can be anything that makes you uncomfortable most of the time

But I believe one of the worst diseases of all

Is the disease to please

Spending most of your time worrying about

What other people think or need

Once you are healed from this

Most of the other diseases will go away too

You will feel so much better

After you start doing what is best for you!

~Life's Tranquilizers~

Life's tranquilizers don't come in a bottle of pills

They come in a Book of 66 called the Gospel

You can have Eternal Refills with this prescription

For it is the POWER OF GOD UNTO SALVATION!

~Testify~

If God has been good to you

You need to testify

Let someone else know that if they have a need that

He will supply

You can write it in a book or pen it in a song

But let someone know that with God they can't go wrong!

~Victory~

The victory comes after what looked like was going to be defeat

Because with God on your side

There is no way that you can be beat!!

#VICTORY, VICTORY, rah, rah, rah!!!

~Inexperienced~

Being inexperienced teaches you to seek wisdom for the knowledge to get an understanding. After all of this you have experience!

~Enthusiasm~

Enthusiasm is a gentle push placed inside of us by God that keeps us focused while completing every assignment that He has given us!

It is our own little inner pep squad yelling… "Give me a one, give me a two, come on now team let's push through…yeahh!!!"

~BOLDNESS~

The same thing that makes the lion to roar fearlessly is the same thing that causes the bear to growl ferociously. It is the same thing that enables you to get back up and continue to fight after being knocked down…it is called BOLD-NESS!

~Corrections~

Corrections are road signs from God that lead us in the right direction. No matter how He may send them it is in our best interest to pay attention!

~Laughter~

Laughter is when you put on and wear sadness inside out. Oh my, it looks good on you! Don't you feel better?

#Hahaha
#Proverbs 17:22

~Emotions~

Emotions come in all colors, shapes, and sizes

Some come in the color blue

Whether or not it looks good on you

Some are high, some are low

Some stay for a little while

Some don't seem to want to go!

~Intercessory Prayer~

Intercessory prayer decreases hell's population

It can reach anyone around the world in any nation

If you have been called to intercede

Believe you me, there is always a need

So please take intercessory prayer seriously

The souls you save will benefit eternally!!!

#I AM AN Intercessor

~Making Memories~

Making memories doesn't take a whole lot of ingredients

Just a pinch of love and kindness

And a dash of time for the seasoning!

~A Kiss~

A kiss is one of the deepest forms of showing passion

Like when a mother first lays her eyes on her newborn baby

Plants a kiss on him or her, then something amazing begins to happen

That kiss speaks a language that is spoken without words

It is the sealing of a bond that can never be broken or destroyed!

~Tenderness~

I truly believe that God created tenderness

It is like a secret ingredient

When put in any medicine will cure whatever has you sick

If man had formulated it, he would ask for a fortune

But God gives it freely when we share it with one another!

~Endurance~

Our endurance is God's assurance that we will make it to the end.

Because it was transfused into us when Jesus shed His Blood on the Cross

So now it pumps and flows through our spiritual veins

So just like Him, we will never be defeated ever again!

~HELL!~

Hell is hot

Whether you believe it or not

Hell is real

Once you are there, you will remain eternally

Hell is forever

There is no leaving, no not ever

Please Don't Go

Repent and Live Holy!!!

~Uninvited~

Some people would agree that it would be very rude to go

To a place where you're uninvited and come walking boldly through the door

But I have discovered, that is exactly what memories do

They come when you least expect them and they linger longer than you ask them to

Thankfully they're not all undesirable and a dread to have around

And some are really comforting

Invited or not they can turn that frown upside down!

~In Between~

As we all know there are twelve months in a year

We never know from one month to the next what could suddenly appear

But one thing for sure we must remember

There's a lot to look forward to between January and December!

~Escape Artist~

If life teaches you one thing

It is how to escape

You will get plenty of experience as you live from day to day

Before this life is over things can get harder and harder

But you can overcome and become a great escape artist!

#I Corinthians 10:13

~Test Time~

Shhh…quiet please test is in session

I'm trying so hard to pass, listening to God for directions

Please be patient with me for God is not through with me yet

But when I finish my tests

What you see will be what you get!

~Hidden Potential~

Children are not the only ones who play hide and seek

Potentials have its own games with many secrets

Sometimes you never know what's hidden inside of you

It's amazing what you will find hidden inside as life takes you through!

~Reflections~

What do I see in the mirror of life

What do I need to change while there is still time

When I look at myself

What do I see

Most of all what does God see when He's looking at me

Do I reflect a life that He is pleased with

When I stand before Him will He say

"Well done my servant!"

~Hurting~

There is a saying that "hurting people hurt people"

But I would like to add that hurting people can also hurt themselves

By failing to love themselves or not forgiving someone else

If you neglect yourself

You will be the one that hurts the most

So do all you can to heal yourself

Stop nursing hurt, just let it go!

~Angels~

It is so wonderful to know

That God shares with us His Friends

They are known by the name of Angels and

Will be with us until the very end

Sometimes they are disguised as strangers

So be careful how you entertain them

Because thy could very well be Angels!

~Baggage~

Why are you still carrying baggage from the past

You need to get rid of it and do it fast

The longer it takes

The more it will accumulate

And you will never get where you need to be

With all that unnecessary weight!

~Be Rare~

Being real is very rare

You won't find it often and most certainly not
everywhere

So choose to be a priceless commodity

And be real for real

Make the world much better and a more genuine
place to live!

~Silent Generation~

No matter what time and era that you were born

Don't become silent but continue to sound the
alarm

Make a loud noise of love

Shout it in the air

Let everyone that meet know that you really do care!

~Appreciation~

What does it mean to appreciate

Believe me it's something very wonderful, make no mistake

To show this to someone is like taking a dream vacation

So make someone's dream come true

Show them some appreciation!

~Bye-Bye!~

These two words can be very hard to say

To someone whose welcome is up and they no longer need to stay

They were only meant to be in your life for only a season

Not for a lifetime, or any other reason

Chances are they will pretend that they don't know why

That you suddenly and finally decided to tell them bye-bye

But trust me when I say that it is time for them to go

So just open up and let them out of your heart's door

Don't let them make you think that they can't be replaced

Because God has someone for you that will fill that lonely and empty space!

~Open Book~

I once lived my life very private and reserved

I was going through so much that I felt I didn't deserve

Chapter after chapter of my life was an unhappy ending

I would often wonder what it would be like to have a new beginning

Then as God would have it to be

On a page of one of the chapters were the words written "Why don't you really TRUST ME"

So as I applied these words and began to regroup

I now can live my life as an open book!

~Limited Edition~

Extra, Extra, Read All About It!

I'm living proof that life can be exciting

I know that's a headline that you don't often see

Hurry, get your copy

It's a limited edition!

~The End~

If we could fast forward our life to the end

We would miss the opportunity to learn so much about life in between

Yes some of life's lessons come with a great cost

But God makes sure that nothing is wasted or lost

So make the best of this life and live it with grace

So at The End you will hear the Lord say

"Well Done, you ran a great race!"

A Message From The Author

What you have experienced from reading Inspirational Hugs for Living, is a very uniquely written, nonfictional novel that is based on real characters and actual events.

The form and style is different from your usual novel but the message and meaning is a real life story with all of life's challenges, both negative and positive. These challenges have allowed me to grow and become stronger and better and to help others do the same!

I can now relate to everyone who God allows to come across my path on this life's journey and to do so with compassion and Much Love.

These nuggets and hugs are about me, The Author, and all that I have Lived to Learn and Learned to Live…

Yours Truly,

Special Thanks

To some of the actual characters that were portrayed in the book:

Stephanie Nicole Lackey as "The Lion" in the "The Lion and The Lamb"

Stacey Neshon Lackey as "The Lamb" in "The Lion and the Lamb"

www.ingramcontent.com/pod-product-compliance
Lightning Source LLC
Chambersburg PA
CBHW051956090426
42741CB00008B/1418